ALL FIRE   ALL WATER

Books by Judith Roche

All Fire All Water
Wisdom of the Body
First Fish First People: Salmon Tales of the North Pacific Rim
Myrrh/ My Life as a Screamer
Ghosts

ALL FIRE ALL WATER

Judith Roche

Black Heron Press
Post Office Box 13396
Mill Creek, Washington 98082
www.blackheronpress.com

Some of the poems in *ALL FIRE ALL WATER* have appeared in these journals and publications: *Muse:An International Journal of Poetry, Manoa Journal, Windfall, The Far Field, About Place Journal, Faultlines, Platte River Review, Malpais Review, Skagit River Festival Anthology, Raven Chronicles.* The Brightwater poems are installed at the Brightwater Treatment Plant, thanks to the generous support of 4Culture, King County, Washington's commission for the arts.

ISBN-13: 978-1-936364-16-9
ISBN-10: 1-936364-16-6

Black Heron Press
Post Office Box 13396
Mill Creek, Washington 98082
www.blackheronpress.com

CONTENTS

THE HUSBANDS SWEET

WE ARE STARDUST

RIVERS HAVE MEMORIES

UPRIVER, THE SKAGIT

Here swiftly,
amid broken boulders
house-sized and strewn
far below the high cascade
descending almost from heaven,
amid the swirl and rush of water
dashing down and filling
the scatter of river-gouged pools,
broken necklace of moonstones
frothing at my feet, terraced
between brimming
turbulence of tumbled stone
slung from who-knows-where–
Anchorage, the Arctic–
volcanic events of rocks
unstrung and exploding
in the abyss
before beginnings,
before we had names,
to hesitate only briefly
in this watershed,
a moment on tiptoe
of geological time,
before clattering on
and the water rushing
down down down.

VERNAL EQUINOX

A green wind rushes
over cold ground, freshening

what's left of winter slush.
Trees gush song,

blush crimson
gold stipples,

extending branches.
Persephone returns.

Her rejoicing mother
starts seeds and tubers

rumbling underground,
teeming with life.

Daffodil and hyacinth erupt,
unfueling sweet scent of spring,

a row of wild onions takes fire
from the new moon.

Pale green pea tendrils
push out of bare earth

and the wounded god
will walk the land,

whole again, becoming
radiant with resurrection.

NEIGHBORHOOD NEWS

Mary's goat has been rescued from the roof
and grazes in high parts of the pasture—
the flood left lowlands still soaked with sog.
Her neighbor's cow drowned in the barn,

hundreds of Iowa homes swept away or trashed,
and snakes are swimming in the basements.
But Mary's out there (game girl that she is),
helping the Mennonites fill sandbags.

They all call her "author lady"
and are happy for the help. The National Guard is out,
but most of them are in Iraq by now. Mary says,
"If you have an emergency, call the Mennonites."

On the Left Coast we've had a cold spring
and our berry crop has failed, but the East Coast
sweltered and melted like tea cakes in the sun.
In Ohio, David and Vanessa had to pack up the babies

and head to the basement when a tornado
blew through, but the house is okay.
And 40,000 acres of California is burning
in 1,400 separate fires, not enough water to fight.

The Feds cut ships for climate research
to save fuel, at the price of gas these days.
The headline named it Catch 22,
and noted they hadn't yet named a ship The Irony.

THE CRANES
Platte River, Nebraska

The sound comes first,
wild and wind-born,
a kind of purling purr
deep from long throats,
larynxes that can bend and twist,
but cranes fly with necks outstretched,
legs and feet streaming long behind,
chambers in the throat reverberating
sound to a thrum, strange
song, a madrigal, together,
voices in a fugue.

Then the sight – long skeins;
strings stretched over the river–
not a flock, but threaded out,
one after the other, seemingly
unending, pouring out across
the river in almost endless flow,
a waterfall of river fowl
to settle in shallow waters
edging sandbars, the better
to hear coyote, fox, bobcat
splashing towards them.

Lean and lovely they come, redheaded and hungry–
stop and fuel for the long flight home.

In crepuscular light,
silver and darkening.
We are cold in the bird blind,
a mean wind creeps around
corners and between cracks,
knotting our fingers and toes,
but we must stay until they
settle. Finally it's too dark
to see – we make our way out,
single file, away from the river.
Silence. And hope.

THE CONTINENT OF PLASTIC
turning and turning in the widening gyre

it swirls beneath the surface on ocean currents
massive vortex

new kind of wetland
bobbing and shifting

on no fixed boundaries
roiling reflection of a billion million

stars in the Milky Way
undulating tidewoven flow

swirling and gleaming like Van Gogh's Starry Night,
tooth brushes, plastic bags, fishing nets

shoelace tips, water bottles, broken toys,
condoms blasted to bits by sun and waves

this eighth entity kills
inhabitants and visitors alike–

sea-turtles mistake plastic produce bags
for filmy jelly-fish

krill and plankton feeders suck it in
sea birds gorge on fragments–

plastic pearls looking like fish eggs –
and regurgitate

into the waiting mouths
of hungry chicks.

FISHTOWN, LOWER SKAGIT
from a long canoe with 18 paddlers
"Language burned in us. We were wild with ideas…"
—Bob Rose

Water rocks under us.
Water pours over us, from a slate sky.
Water collects in the bottom of the boat,
drips off our hat brims, soaks through our clothes.

Purple larkspur shows vivid against rain-blackened
rock faces. Columbine in niches clings in shallow soil,
saxifrage shines white on succulent stems.
A red-tailed hawk drifts above, looking for lunch.

We rock in the river's current, *"Paddles ready,"*
then *"all paddles ahead,"* and *"Paddles rest,"*
shouted from the back of the boat. A mean
wind arrives from the south. We're pilgrims searching

the ghost of Fishtown hovering in this Skagit rain,
but most shacks have been torn down,
the land logged, leaving bare bones, or nothing but green.
The hopeful artists and scholars of the estuary

scattered, mostly still around the valley, still making art.
All in our sixties and seventies now.
Some have passed, a life lived for art –as ephemeral as a dance–
but many leave a trail of poems and paintings behind.

None can quite leave behind the life lived on the Skagit,
the youthful hope and dedication.

Shacks, landmarks and channels gone.
But *"Rivers have memories,"* says Bob Rose. Restless, they adjust

in their beds. Robert Sund is gone but his tight little cabin
is a refuge from today's rain. We huddle inside
and crowd around the wood stove, drink hot tea and listen
to Tim McNulty read Sund's poems of this place. Water,

water, herons, rain, swallows, mud, and rain again.
Even a former resident of Fishtown can't find
what was there. The river has changed channels
and Fishtown, a state of mind.

THE WOLVES OF WASHINGTON STATE

A breeding pair of wolves
roams the ridges, cubs
tumbling in their den.

Welcome to the land's insistent
voice echoing in spirals
from the North, howling

across the Teanaway again.
After many years and terrors
the wolves know their time

has come to this land again.
With the patience of the wild
they've waited for this call and response

a cappella canon. Songbirds trill
their return. Aspens tremble gratitude
and flourish now as elk

browse lightly but move on.
Ravens, magpies, jays, crows,
vultures thank good fortune,

for kill they can pick clean—
bloody leaving of our wolves,
tearing canines, unfortunate prey.

Shattered white bones scatter wolf
scat – a lamb's shank, a deer or elk's skull,
now and again a trusted dog's bones.

Ranchers wring their hands
and go for their guns. Guard
dogs have ancestral dreams.

Polyphonic howls
climb the steep mountain,
slide down the valley's slope.

TAHQUAMENON NORTH

"When we can take the most Northerly route
I'm happy," my sister says. The children
yapped in the back seat. I had to buy
a new map to show them our progress.

And we drove further North into a crisp late summer,
stopped at Tahquamenon, foaming root beer falls.
Tannins steeped from tree roots, we learned.
Birch, spruce, hemlock and swamp cedar. .

Now in all the stores we stopped along the way
sheet rock gave way to knotty pine
and mounted animal heads—
moose, bear and big cat.

A white wolf's hide on the wall
at our lunch stop. My sister shuddered.
I scanned the highway margins
for deer and saw coyote

feeding on road kill, and 'possum, mostly raccoons.
My sister identified a circling vulture
by his arched eyebrow wings. A raven.
The backseat cubs nipped and batted at each other.

We stopped to watch the rivers
run by and by and by, circling the earth,
saw a lump of scat on the trail,
laced with scatter of white bones.

MELISSA

One moment, then the plunderer slips
Between the purple flower-lips
Hymen, H.D.

They visit my garden,
dive into mauve and magenta,
crimson and cerise.
They dip into lady slippers,
climb the foxglove,
honeysuckle, hibiscus,
to sip the sweetness
warmed loam breeds
from death-rot and seed.

Their gold-dusted bodies
pour out an amber
to match the sun's splendor,
mellifluous nectar for themselves
and liquid gold to give us.

Good neighbors, they carry
hostess gifts on tiny legs
and visit often to help the harvest.
They dance a precise vocabulary,
measure the angle from the sun
for degree and direction
to the fairest flowers,
choreograph a chart of earth
and calculate distance
in kinetic circles and spirals,
dancing bodies accompanied
by the thrum

of their winged music.
            Pagans all, they worship a Queen.
            and know the princely lovers
            courting her must die.

BEE VILLANELLE

To make a prairie it takes a clover and one bee,/
One clover, and a bee,/And revelry. — Emily Dickinson

They were with us so long
Heavy with gold-dusted bodies they go.
We'll miss their sibilant song.

Could it be that pesticides are all wrong?
Their honey, their pollen–no one seems to know.
They were with us so long.

March to September, half said so long.
US, Europe, Guatemala, Brazil, so
silence descends on their sibilant song.

They rise up and fly off in a mighty throng,
Some even say a Rapture in the meadow.
They were with us so long.

People are puzzled, worldwide strong.
This year farm crops will cast a thin shadow.
We'll miss their sibilant song.

Has the Great Bee Queen heard her evensong?
In all climates, from sun to snow.
They were with us so long.
We miss their sibilant song.

AUTUMN TWILIGHT

The witch is in her kitchen
stirring up a soup.
The crow is in his treetop,
summoning up a storm.
The storm is in the stratosphere
muscling up her sinew.
The rain is on the rooftop
throbbing out a song.
The river runs her riverbanks
swelling all along.
And I am in my cedar house
staring at the lessening light,
going going gone.

The witch is feeding elves and trolls
The crow is flying higher.
The storm may dissipate or not,
depending on the weather.
The elves and trolls begin to eat
a rank and unidentified meat.
The river's flowing on and on.
But the twilight is still creeping,
going going gone.

WOLF AT THE DOOR

The wind is howling at the door,
putting to shame his cousin
who harassed the Three Little Pigs.
Crash! — there goes another big tree branch.
Bang! — that's probably a whole tree
down in the dell.
Crackle! — that's surely the power line
because now I'm in the dark,
pointlessly clicking at light switches.

Soon the cold creeps in, obsequious,
its slow encroachment silently sliding
through doors I should have
weather-stripped, then later,

a full-frontal attack on the broadside
of inadequately insulated walls.
I've built a fire but the thermometer
drops dramatically, the cold now running
amuck and the dark thickens.

The fragile infrastructure supporting us,
thin, naked as we are without a pelt
to protect. The cat doesn't mind.
He can even see in the dark all my candles
barely penetrate. Even other primates
have enough coat and I'm miserable *indoors*.

But there's plenty of souls out there,
huddled under Seattle bridges, for whom
the cold is a nightly routine, though this
huffing and puffing wolf is unique to tonight.
The battery-operated radio says
days until we're re-connected
to power, for even the powerful
in their lakeside mansions.
On this cold night, a forced equality.

DECEMBER STORM

Water and wind all night.
I wake and worry about a tree
poised over my house
while visions of undulance writhe in my head.
The wind roars like the creature it is
and trees pitch and rage an angry answer.
My bed is a boat to carry me through
the wild hours and I toss
on the waves of the tempest.

DECEMBER, LAKE WASHINGTON

Dry moon dust sifts out
a tiny puncture wound in the skin
of the moon and scatters
its shining self on lake's liquid
and lithe surface tension
to shimmer her path of cold light
on this late December night.

BRIGHTWATER

Note: The Brightwater Water Treatment Plant is part of King County's regional system that treats wastewater for about 1.5 million people and covers 420 square miles in the Puget Sound region. The following three poems are installed at the Brightwater site as public art, thanks to 4Culture, the cultural services agency for King County, Washington. *Blessings for Brightwater* and *no beginning...*is part of an art piece by Jane Tsong, titled *...no beginning no end/circle the earth/blessed water/blood of life...*

Litany for Bright Water is part of 4Culture's temporary art installations for Brightwater. Grateful thanks to 4Culture for their generous support.

no beginning no end

circle the earth

blessed water

blood of life

30

BLESSINGS FOR THE BIOSOLIDS

… for the journey of nutrients
from food to feces,
to compost and back again
to eggplant parmesan, or tabouli.

Blessings for helpful microbes,
mixing juices and decay,
their messy business of heating,
eating, discarding, transforming

one thing to another,
the fetid to the fragrant,
from waste to muck,
to rich soil for the fields.

Blessings for the biosolids,
whose elements began in burning
spheres of ancient star systems, born
of crucibles of burning light.

Praise for minerals new-mined
from stars, connecting any one of us
to Nefertiti, Joan of Arc, Attila the Hun,
Chief Sealth, salmon, centipedes:

carbon-based creatures all,
certainly the stuff of stars.
Blessings for the mighty microbes
within the core of us.

Blessing for the black gold
of rich compost, new-cleansed,
by heat and broken down
by fungi and bacteria, dried,

transformed, now, sweet and loamy,
trucked to wheat fields
of The Palouse, to fertilize
our daily bread.

Blessings for the earthy cycle
from food to waste to humus
and back again to food. Blessings

LITANY FOR BRIGHT WATER

Praise the unbroken cycle of connective pipes,
      veins and arteries in the long body of earth,
      labyrinth of influent/effluent
      swirling to the great heart of the system.

Praise the "archeology of pipes,"
      twists and turns, river connections of conveyance,
      the twine and slide of intricate conjugation.

Praise the vast pump station along
      the line, throbbing the flow
      to and from the cleansing plant,
      connecting a moving river.

Praise human responsibility–
      the ability to respond–
      to mend and amend damage we create,
      to restore an ancient balance.

Praise trucks that carry the cleansed away
      over our mountains to nourish the fields,
      waste no longer wasted
      but returned, clean and useful.

Praise water, now clear and shining,
      revivifying the water cycle,
      out to the fields,
      and on home to Puget Sound.

Praise rain sinking in groundwater,
     taken up by sweet winds,
     wetland reclaimed and home to nesting deer,
     raccoon, frogs, blue herons,
     coyote, river otter – all the soul of the woods.

Praise trees returning, covered in glossy feathers,
     bright song, skies of winged flight,
     pathways where sudden flash of sliding snake
     surprises our sight.

Praise deep roots in the earth, branching and spreading,
     braided pathways for life-giving water.

Praise the tangle of waterways, passage for salmon,
     No Name Creek, Little Bear Creek, the Sammamish,
     on to Lake Washington and out to the Salish Sea.

Praise our shining Salish Sea,
     to which our water returns,
     completing the cycle.

A BIRD CAUGHT IN THE THROAT

ARCANE EXPOSITIONS

like peacocks stepping out of cages into an
empty kitchen of God —Anne Carson

Another word for terror is a bird caught in the throat.
Another word for now is black bits of paint flaking off.
They fly away in a flock and settle down with slit tongues.

Many women die in childbirth in a hail of stones.
Many children catch those stones, debris falling like shooting stars.
Another word for desert is the rain dreams fire
      and falls in a red lake.

We have dreaded this like death—
      we knew it was coming.
Oil flows fast in the rivers,

and old truths come to life
presaged by rivers on fire and acid hailstones,
tessellated out into its logical conclusion.

Another word for wilderness is honey in the comb.
Another word for bees is black and gold song.

Another word for greed is teeth bite
off a piece of ass. It could be anybody's.

Another word for form is cabbages roasted in ash
taking the shape of a human body.

Another word for us is a cluster of chromosomes.
Another word for gravity is the love of home.

There are no synonyms.
Another word for now is the walls come tumbling down.

THE FACE OF WAR

Sing, Divine Muses, of the ruinous wrath of Achilles
—Homer

With polyphonic voices, we sing
the horror of these mutilated cities
where immortal cruelty roams

our halls and pathways, punctuated
by beauty, shafts of light
slatting through our ribs. We follow bloody

footsteps down corridors of fallen feathers
past clusters of gathered flowers
rotting in the stench of neglect.

A small child wanders in the debris.
Somewhere the mother is torn apart
and no one has found the imagination

to bury her broken body.
Somewhere the father is busy
with his work, killing other children,

though he prays for his own,
now lost in a ruined house.
The river fattens with rotted bodies.

The rain weaves a dense shroud
heavy with the weight of grief.
The young, excited by the sheer energy

of moving parts, meshing and unmeshing,
hear screams of metallic song
in a streaming sunset, black and crimson.

The old know we have been here before,
making the same wrong turns.
The dead turn their backs,

haunting the road.
The songs turn and turn again,
slit the throat of night and spill over,

returning like rhyme,
 extended vowels,
howling the same note.

HEART

It's a hollow vessel
that must host a river at flow

or die. The four rooms of come and go,
doors opening and closing, high and low.

Our core, *coeur*, circulating calls
out for ease on an odd bridge.

Soul spider flings strings to a land we might fail to find,
muscular dance in concentric circles of heavy loss.

It's an attack that might come, a burn,
scalding sensibility, which might break

us finally, or bring fragrant scent
of woods violets and wild ginger,

depending on how the wind might blow,
and the smell of the soul.

The heart—lion or lily—wants what it wants
and will not be denied.

The song could be a Puccini aria
or Robert Johnson blues, the background of the bargain.

DETAINEES SCARRED BY IMPRISONMENT
YEARS AFTER RELEASE

Yet as the old Greek said/We walk on the
faces of the dead —Sam Hamill

Weeding my garden I poked my eye with a sharp weed.
My face got wet (tears from pain, I thought).

When the dripping reached my chin I brushed it away
and the back of my hand came away bloody.

Last Sunday, in church, my friend told me
she wouldn't mind going to Hell if she could

supervise the circle where they put
those who are cruel to animals.

What would she do with them?
I'm trying to see through a veil of bloody tears.

When my eyes cleared I went to Danté to find which circle
my friend would be assigned to. The Seventh is set aside

for the violent, the first ring of the Seventh Circle supervised
by Centaurs, shaggy horse-men who shoot arrows

at those who try to climb out of their river of hot blood
farther than their guilt allows. But at the corners lurks

the Minotaur, another half-beast-half man,
a recipient of much cruelty in his own short life,

some say deservedly (he *did* eat the children),
but he stalked the stonewalls of his labyrinth

alone and hungry and knew no compassion in life.
Here he bellows, bites and gnaws his own arm,

turning his pain in on himself, poor beast.
Perhaps the Centaurs are as in a dream

all aspects of the dreamer so the guilty punish
themselves by their own awareness of their cruelty.

Some stand only ankle deep in boiling blood
and others are submerged to their eyes.

The doctor says I will have no permanent damage,
though, having once bled from the eye

I will always see differently
Abu Ghraib, Guantanamo Bay,

Guatemala, Pinochet's Chile, College
of the Americas to teach the craft.

And for the turtle I found as a child and saw boys
beat him to death, my first sight of deliberate cruelty.

My sister and I buried him in a vacant lot,
but the boys dug him up and beat him some more.

My sister sobbed to our mother,
"Oh, Mama, his poor dirty little eyes!"

Would my friend torture the torturers back?
She tells me, "Some would."

HOFFA

That day a substitute appeared in history, a stranger,
reading the roll and stumbling over unfamiliar surnames
full of aspirants and strange combinations of diphthongs.
It was mid-century Detroit and we were a mixed bunch.

I remember her coming to a boy's name,
the unhealthy gleam of almost prurient curiosity,
"Hoffa?" she pounced. "Are you the son?" aloud, and loud,
Every child and teacher in Cooley High School knew

this boy was the son of the famous name, which shrilled
in bold type on our nightly newspapers.
Miss K, of the Polish name with many consonants,
our real teacher, would not have made the boy talk about it.

We were in the eleventh grade, what did we know
of adults' intrusive probing in an open wound?
We were only beginning to learn of adult agendas.
We were not quite blanks but still growing the faces we would become.

The boy just said "Yes." The kids leaned in,
held their collective breath, embarrassed for the boy.
"Well, what does your father think about the newspapers?"
she pressed, an itching in her voice. "And is he guilty?"

We were in the eleventh grade for such a short time,
were just learning the meaning of the word *grace*.
We were beginning to grow language in abstraction
like chin hairs and new breasts, though most of us could not yet

have used *grace* in connection with a kid in our class.
But the boy found it in his answer. He said it was not part of history yet,
so beyond the realm of the class.
I told the story at home. My father just rattled his paper.

"I don't believe what they say," my mother finally said.
"They've been through his life with a fine-toothed comb
and can find no murder to pin on him, nothing to prove."
When that father did go to prison, it was not for murder but tax evasion.

My mother would say they could prove nothing worse.
"And," my mother continued, "he's never been unfaithful to Josephine."
The wife. My mother would care about that.
"That ought to count for something."

It was Detroit. Snow fell, ice ringed bare tree branches in winter.
Political dynasties fell and rose. Labor unions gained strength, then lost it.
Winter and summer, in Midwestern contrast, continued. History
is the water we drink from the shallow footsteps of memory.

Years later, in Alaska, where we got few newspapers,
we got the one that said that father had disappeared,
presumed murdered. I closed my eyes, for grief–
my high school friend, his sister, and Josephine.

The story goes on, as they all do, for those left.
For years the father's disappearance became
a national joke–on talk shows and comics' routines.
And still is. Cement shoe jokes, common

in Detroit, New York, Chicago. Funny to some.
I've seen the son on national television
here and there, over the years. James, the son, graying,
as I am, looking more and more like Jimmy, the father,

now matured into the dignity
he found first in the eleventh grade.

YESTERDAY/TODAY

Yesterday, the broken heart of the world
opened and allowed the great rains down.
Sorrow, holding tight, unfurled.

Last leaves lost their grip and swirled
to litter sodden on the ground.
Yesterday the broken heart of the world

was overwhelmed, too sore
to hold. But today's sky found
light again. Something held tight, unfurled,

forgot abused children, cruelty and war
– if only for a minute – the sound
of the broken heart of the world.

Madly glorious, November warmth curled
down on amber autumn, surprising all around.
Sorrow, holding tight, unfurled.

Today, some pain tore
open and golden sun crowned.
Yesterday the broken heart of the world,
sorrow, held tight, unfurled.

THE HUSBANDS SWEET

All this hunger is what we call the World
–Fred Wah

THE HUSBANDS SUITE

each an etude in which I lay to learn
something technical but played for artistry

a string and a strand, a block and a battery
the bitter bundled in the honey'd swarm

vacations of vacant vocations
the flung over-the-shoulder

fare-thee-well
exercises in experience
more expensive than I can tell.

FIRST

The way we begin is at my wedding.
An older cousin tells me
I am beautiful, the way
a woman is most, as a bride
       –or newly pregnant–
I am both.
       Now I know
for the first time
there is a small cluster
of cells rocking
in the boat of my belly
underneath creamy satin, ivory lace.
She floats within
on a still-calm saline sea.

I've avoided knowing
until this moment
       but already
the hieroglyphics of genetics
are sketching out her flame-
colored hair, her nose,
unfurling the curvilinear
line of her sacrum,
knitting the eggs
which will become
my grandchildren,
and igniting the ardent flame
she will be born with.

I yearn toward her
for the first time,
but I don't know yet
how hard
it will be to keep
her safe.

THE HUSBANDS

I married them for all the wrong reasons.
One for sex, another for a boat,
though the boat wasn't for me
but for the son left behind
from the sex I married the first one for.
But it was the daughter I carried inside
when I married the first one.
There were others but they
didn't quite count as husbands.

The third I didn't even marry.
He read me poems in bed
and left little behind, nothing of any value.
But the pain turned out about the same.
And then there was my daughter,
steady, there through all of it,
watching me with blue owl eyes,
thinking, is this the way you do it?

We had boat enough to teach us
of the sea, the beauty of fish,
the son's love for water.
The first left me my daughter and my son,
both, my dawn, noon, sunset, and night.

The husbands are all far away now,
two into that great good night–
strange to have outlived them.
The third, off in his own mysteries.
They surface in my dreams,

sometimes even the others join in,
as lions, as kings, as husbands.
They all blend together, vivid,
purring loudly and shape shifting.
I love them – or him –
the one Great Husband,
for whom I am still a wife.

POSTCARDS FROM WATER

"..in the ghost canyon of memories..." —Jack Spicer

There was a boat on the shore
and we set out in it.
Pull pull, pull pull,
through drag,
the weight of water.
We don't know
where we go.
Love in a lifeboat,
we could go beyond
maps and off the shelf
of the known earth.

Dear Mick,
in this card you have turned your back on me.
Typical, when I wanted you to pay attention.
But you paid too much attention when I didn't want it.
Dear Mick, I'm sorry for your sorrow and relieved to be free.
Dear Mick, our children are doing fine, but bereaved
of a father. Bereaved of boats.

The river is iced—
cars can drive across.
What does that have to do with me?

Summer on the water,
sun and sparkle.
Summer at the cottage
with no shoes.

Winter and wind-sculpted
great hills of piled up
frozen water. We walked out
a long way–much farther
than we could swim in summer.
This is Lake Erie, which leads
to the Detroit River, cars
can drive on it. A dead seagull
iced in. White on white.
What does this have to do with me?

Dear Mother,
in this card you have taken me to the art museum again.

Once I told a man my main relationship with my mother
was through art and literature and he found it tragic.
Not so, Dear Mother, you gave me a world beyond the hard-worked
streets of our mid-century industrial city and stifled ideas.
Dear Mother, the children grew up strong and fine,
but bereaved of a grandmother. I tried to tell the stories
but didn't do it as well as you.

Dear River,
cars drive on your surface,
a tunnel flows under the water,
another country, the other side...

When we rode through the tunnel
as children, we ducked our heads and laughed.

We drove across the bridge, my young husband
and I, on the way to the cottage,
and summer on Lake Erie,
babies in the backseat.

Dear Ice,
the rum-runners crossed
on your surface. Some booze-loaded cars
broke through and drowned. Some
rusted hulks still at the bottom. What
does this have to do with me?

Dear River,
It's said the Lakes never
give up their dead.
Do you, Dear River,
know the names of your dead?

Dear Road,
I've traveled you from the City of the Straits, Day-twa
and far beyond. My father taught me how.
I wrapped the river around me like a scarf,
immersed myself in the Great Lakes, sweeter
than the sea. I come from you. My young husband

taught me how, before the sorrow
that overtook us. Dear Road,
what do you have to do with me?

Dear Roadside Flowers,
Queen Anne's Lace, Pearly Everlasting.

Dear Diana of the Hunt,
where have your lean hunting hounds gone,
the blue tick and the black and tan? They bugle
in the distance, a clean clear song.

Dear Father, Dear Uncles,
you gave me the hounds.

Dear Hounds,
You gave me the night.

Dear River,
I come home to you. There is a boat on the shore,
we set out in it. The drag, the weight of water, sweet water.

Dear Salish Sea,
Saline, not sweet, astringent. Phosphorescence
shines on you, I set out.

HUSBANDS DREAM

We dream – it is good we are dreaming–
It would hurt–were we awake   —Emily Dickinson

Last night I had both husbands,
one in a travel trailer and one
in an empty swimming pool
where I was mucking out
deep mud at the bottom.
With the travel-trailer-husband
I was getting a cabin ready
to close for the winter,

both of us turning things off
for the coming cold.
With the swimming-pool-husband,
my mother was there too,
cooking a thanksgiving turkey.
Deep mud at the bottom,
closed for the winter.
A stage stood at one end of the pool

where I was planning a theater
for deaf children come spring,
which didn't come.
The jumble of husbands,
one in a travel trailer,
children in an empty swimming pool,
rattled around in my head,
lurching up against the force of history,

stumbling over its own mysteries,
trying to birth itself in a blood soup
of phonemes in a murky pool.
What does it mean? I asked my mother.
But I couldn't hear
her answer from the travel trailer.
I was driving in reverse on a narrow road
with such dense foliage it kept scratching the car.

Night so dark the rear-view mirror
couldn't find light to reflect.
I had to hang my head
out the window to see where I'd been,
driving backward, I couldn't hear my mother
and the foliage kept smacking me
in the face. The husbands had disappeared
by then and couldn't help,

stumbling over their own mysteries.
The theater for deaf children didn't come
in the spring. I had to hang my head.

STORY AND VARIATIONS

Did I leave him for a Classics professor
from Chapel Hill or did he leave me for a Plain
Jane of a girl? Wind-chill became a factor.
There were children involved. The Classics professor
lasted about a minute. The plain girl pined
at the window a long time. He flew to the wild blue.
We continued to pass children back and forth. I found
a man with a rose between his teeth. Classic. But he
didn't know the Classics. I left the man with the rose
after our tango frazzled, my slit skirt crumpled,
classically. In time he left the girl who pined. He flew
ever higher until even the children didn't ground him.
We kept missing each other at assigned assignations.
Georgian Bay, lichens living on rock- how could they be
nourished? Puerto Rico, paella in the café and tears flourished.
Ocean beaches where we walked so far we lost our car.
A motorcycle trip of wind and rain, dangerous. Rain
hits your face like little pellets of shot. We learned
to lean into the turns, then forgot. The girl who pined
at the window ended up alone.
And so did he, flying solo. The man with the rose
tangoed himself to a tangle of fatal temptations.
The children grew the best they could, considering.
We should have plotted out the story
before we passed through. We should
have watched where we were going.

ELECTION 2004

And that night
when the red states kept
overwhelming the blue,
he curled up in his chair
in front of the TV and said
     "no more four years."

In the morning his roommate
found him, still curled in his chair.
Not unusual. A bottle of Courvoisier
empty beside him. Not unusual.
In the evening the housemate
coming home, found him still and cold,
exactly curled into his chair.

Years before, in detox,
he shook and trembled, cold to the bone.
I brought him my son's sweater.
He thanked me then, though
I had much more to thank him for—
in the complicated way we buy
both our affections
and our forgiveness,
a tangle of what we pay
for what we get in a marriage.

We did what we could
though it was too late
to give what he needed,

which had always,
in spite of his kindness,
been impossible.

This time we sent him on his way
with prayers and candle light,
deep red roses filling the house—
                an echo of those he used to bring me.

YELLOW TULIPS

Sunday morning
sun flaring through
my kitchen window,
sun-struck tulips
on my breakfast table
have spread themselves
wide open,
showing everything
they've got inside,
which they've kept
hidden for days.

He does a dramatic
double-take, turning
from scrambled eggs
on a white plate,
and asks their sun-splashed
loveliness, "You girls from Texas?"
in a smoky singles-bar kind of voice.
I remember what he said
last night, bobbing
in the boat of my tangled bed,
  "A man could kill over a cunt
but he can die for a pussy."

ASSIGNATION EAST OF THE MOUNTAINS

Swerving through sculpted hills
naked and rounded greengold-shadowed,
and driving
a powerful engine surging over eighty
when I wasn't looking.
It was red and rented,
neither yours nor mine.
Exhilarated by the guilty us-ness
of us, I sail up and over
Snoqualmie Pass, across Denny Creek Bridge
with the Rolling Stones,
loud and nasty as the work it took
to build that bridge.

Actually, I did build that bridge,
in what seems like former life,
me and the construction cowboys
who know how to dance
better than they can talk,
throwing themselves into sinew-straining,
bone-buckling work to lose
themselves in the action
of the moment, like dancing,
or sex, the intensity
making us forget who we are,
become pure body running
hard, sweating, the joy in the doing
not the done, a singing in the blood,
at one with the physics of the body,
its gears and meshes, movable parts,

slick and oiled, responding
to whatever is asked of us.

I used to work and drink
with them, on the mountain
and in a bar in North Bend,
and now I'm driving
across this bridge in a rented car,
blinding light and gritty music, loud and
sun glittering off snowy mountain tops,
engaged as I ever have been,
in speed and moving,
both toward and away from
your body, this dance.

DO NOT DISTURB

You're in the basement
sorting sodden detritus
from last spring's disaster
and counting up the costs
when he calls from Cincinnati.
"I want to tell you where I've been,"
he offers. "Please,"
you say, "don't bother.'
The costs are still mounting
as your hands go on handling
drenched draperies beginning
to stench of mold and old LP's
silted with stuck-to-them sleeves.
He chuckles, and your mind floods
with memory, that little laugh
when bile rose to his brain,
or sorrow, or shame – and you search
through your own cafeteria
of memory to try to name
what begins to rise in you
where it come from
and where it goes.
He hears your hesitation
and his voice softens to a whisper.
Your left hand slides over
your belly, across to the curve
of your waist, and down-
ward to your hips.
"Are we there yet?" he asks.

TRAIN FROM DETROIT

From a fort called Ponchartrain
The City of Detroit became,
my fourth-grade-first-written poem,
for my city's 250-year birthday.
Day-twa, City of the Straits,
water road between two large lakes,
road for those long lake freighters.
Only place in the US where you go south,
by tunnel or bridge, to get to Canada.

Slow travel past boarded windows, broken
green glass, grimed towers, rounded
stone and old brick smoke stacks,
dumped tires beside slow train tracks,
sumac and goldenrod poke through trackside soot.

In a large playfield attached to a school,
burned weeds and barbed wire on low buildings.
Six cop cars swarm two men in handcuffs.
The men could be my long-gone uncles
or my absent and unborn brothers.
The cops, replicas of an evil uncle-in-law
my mother told bad stories about.

A Detroit cop, he handcuffed a black man
and pushed him face-first down the stairs.
These things happened. This was Detroit.
The uncle listened, rapturous, with tears
streaming to soaring opera on the radio—
with passion that would have embarrassed

my Appalachian uncles or French Canadian father—
a passion I aspired to in my life,
so I believed this uncle a finer cut than the rest,
until my mother's story.

Scud-gray sky hangs heavy out of the city
as we pick up speed. Smoke stacks morph
into blue aluminum siding of the closed Cadillac plant.
Now a neighborhood, newer brick, more trees,
now the Dearborn Ford plant, shiny glass box,
now downriver dead car and truck graveyards,
trailer parks and trashy houses,

with wheeling birds sweeping circles overhead,
becoming fallow fields ringed by tall poplar borders,
our double track suddenly blossoming to a wide switchyard
with braided tracks woven into acres of steel mesh.

Past the Ypsilanti Ford Plant, where my sister once worked,
we cross a machine-cut lake,
red leaves settle into a flat black surface,
pool off the Huron River into Ann Arbor.
Now a riverbank of russet red-browns,
gold and ochre leaves beyond the river,
the track's straight lines criss-cross
the curvy river for miles out of Ann Arbor,
past places where my young husband
and I kissed, before babies, before

years of blood under the bridge.
My heart so full here,
I overflow my cornerstones.

Some trees already bare but surrounded
with a red-gold halo on the ground,
a circle skirt stripped by a rough lover,
a perfect shape of naked limbs above,
How things become so colorful just before they die.

Red barns of rural Michigan anchor
corn flying past in such perfect narrow rows
the field appears animated and marching along
in a kind of bouncy cartoon form—
life imitating a flipbook—
it goes so fast.

RIFT

Night fell from inside
a slab of sky.
I hide in my shoe.

There's a dent in the bed
where laughter lived,
and a voided telephone

where I swallow maps and highlands,
low roads, spine rib and tarsal,
search the memory of a meaning.

Stones do not give me comfort.
I lie down in prepositions
and verbs tire me out.

I light the hearth with a box of wind
and a pirate ship,
little packets of light.

Who among the many I am
is shorn of light?
Rift of song?

Pine bough cherry blossom,
egret and crane.
Where is the join of the joiner?

WE ARE STARDUST

no map

how do we know where we are
when the stars we navigate by
no longer exist

our mothers are dead
taking with them what they knew
our fathers are dead

not that they had a clue
we collect what hard-saved
coordinates we've gathered

like wool from ghost sheep
wisping through our fingers
like the gods' feathers

molting in the wind
in no place at all
ancestors have moved

the boundary stones
ley lines may persist
possibly following underground rivers

and song may activate them
somehow paths do seem
to cross and there we find

what we can
at the crossroads

TRANSLATION

The heart of another is a dark forest. —Willa Cather

1.
The crows gather for congress—
they rattle and caw in the crow tree,

noisy and insistent. And I caw back,
ululating at the boundaries of species,

trying to tell them my secret name,
trying to learn it from them.

Doctor Doolittle talked to the animals.
Saint Francis preached to birds,

rabbits and fish followed him to hear his words
and he bargained with a wolf.

Some say barn animals, cattle, sheep, will speak
in human voice at midnight, Christmas Eve

but I look to speak crow ,
or cat, or horse, crane or salmon.

How must we climb these sounds to something
not known? I am scrambling

hand over hand,
rocks falling around me,

out of the limitations of the word
without a map,

chart, or Rosetta stone
to step from stage to stage.

2.
Light moves through my body but stops at what?
I walk a frozen river to where it becomes water,

fluid and moving and toward gill slits,
the lungs I inherited and the name I was given,

the voice I found myself with,
that bridge of crossing over one language to another,

the syntax of one consciousness for another,
in the mute and moving hands,

echo and sound absorption
or vibrating larynx,

Tell me, is it possible
to love without translation?

PAT AND MARY

for Pat Groom and Mary Huseman

In this dream the dead girls are alive.
Pat swaggers in with characteristic confidence,
crackles with tightly wound energy.
Electric and thin. Her shirt is off,
displaying the green jungle tattooed
broadly across her back, the sinuous black panther
slithering up her spine, across her shoulder
and down her left arm. Her small breasts
exposed, but that's not the focal point
with all that going on in back. Scapulae
spread like muscular wings, almost levitating the girl.
Mary follows, carrying gardening gloves and clippers.

Pat and Mary.
Together for eighteen hard years,
running with the wild girls,
while the jungle grew in increments on Pat's back
until it covered it all. Mary, growing seeds, leaves and seeds
to give them away, what they didn't sell.

In the dream Pat draws a knife deftly down the edge
of the walls. "Not enough cut to hurt much," says Mary.
Just enough to show a thin line of blood.
Pat swipes her finger in the crimson,
paints it on her cheeks. "It's art," says Mary,
which she would say about whatever Pat does.

Pat jumps to the produce section of a supermarket,
perches atop a pyramid of stacked artichokes,

78

directing the dance of the vegetables
under lurid fluorescence.
Mary finds the milk and sucks up a carton.

Last time I visited, Pat lay in bed with a respirator hose
in her nose and showed me two new woodcuts.
Still playing with knives.
Mary showed her tender seedlings under growlights.

Pat died in a motel room, after swallowing a month's medications
and chasing them with whiskey.
Mary stayed with us a year longer, then left
with a bang. A gun in Seward Park.
The wild girls remaining
erected a park bench
there in their names.

LINEAR B

Linear B is a syllabic script that was used for writing My-
cenaean Greek, the earliest attested form of Greek.

They counted sheep
based on tens plus singles.

Wool was important
as was wine.

They counted oxen,
and recorded male and female.

They wrote in syllables,
not words. We are still

      figuring them out. Cumin

mattered, as did the color white,
      as in the island Leuke

where Helen stopped while sailing
to Troy, or Egypt,
      depending
         on the story.
There were stories.
      But told around evening fires
learned and retold as ritual, history,
      prayer and pleasure.

Writing was for laundry lists of goods
      recorded on clay tablets.

They wore linen
    and wool, stored olive oil in amphorae.

They ate figs and fennel and cheese,
    spiked with saffron, gathered from the autumn
        crocus at dawn by young girls.

They painted pictures
    of the harvest.

They interpreted dreams
    and the flight of birds.

Women bled and bedded and birthed.
Men bore swords.

Shepherds herded goats and cattle.

A boy might play a pipe of reed,
a daughter might

        sing a song sounding the way honey tastes,
          dance around the threshing floor

when the work was done.

LINEAR A

*Linear A, early form of writing largely from Crete, has not
yet been linked to any known language.*

Probable child of Cretan Hieroglyphics,
possible mother of Linear B, this mother
and daughter had no common referent.

Linear A is open-throated, clay tablets,
personal objects for prayer,
some written on gold or silver hairpins.

Goats, cows, oxen, yes, numbers, yes,
       but why write
             those on hairpins?

Scholars surmise few words—
       figs and bronze, wool,
        and cloth, wicker baskets,

like those girls used to collect
the stamens of crocus,
wicker baskets brought to altars
holding objects we don't know, sacra.

       Objects
            taboo to be touched except during ceremony.

Could morphemes on gold or silver jewelry
be lists of merchandise?

A strange mother and a barely known daughter.
The mother of no known language,

the daughter whose speech we can know
at least a little. Wild child of a wilder mother.

What did they talk about—or did they
even talk to each other? Was there a mother
tongue that bonded the two?

Bird women and bees on vases.
Lists of goods on clay tablets.
A sealed book.

BURNING GHATS, VARANASI
... the holiest of the seven sacred cities

It's all fire and water here.
When the fire is finished its work, the breastbone of a man,
the pelvis of a woman, left intact .

The oldest son, his head shaved, wearing white, the color
of mourning, gives the bones to the river.
The youngest son does the honors for a mother.

All water and fire here—the burning Ghats, the praying Ghats.
At 3:00 a.m. smoke spreads a sooty horizon over the broad river.
At 6:00 the sun rises a festering red in thick air. Fire and water.

A dead cow drifts by on a sluggish current.
People swim, wash clothes, hair, during the day.
At night, ceremonial fires, sonorous chanting. Thousands gather
                                        at water's edge,

pray, sing and dance amid mounds of marigolds, color of flame,
float lit candles downriver on plastic plates of flowers,
                                        loudspeaker prayers,
singing fills the air, tall flames light the night at river's edge.

At the Burning Ghat, the dead wrapped in ritual cloth
surrounded by marigolds. Cows draw to the fires for warmth.
The fuel, sandalwood for the rich, banyan for the poor.

Those who cannot be burned:
1. children under twelve, pure
2. animals, also pure
3. pregnant woman, pure life inside
4. Holy men
5. lepers, impure

These are weighted with stones and dropped
in the river, final home for the holy.
The river flows on, fires burn.

After two hours of fire, the oldest son takes a sturdy bamboo stick
and breaks open the skull to let the spirit escape,
the rest, swept in the river. Waiting street urchins

pick through leftover litter for gold teeth or earrings
The dead, brought on trains from all of India,
are carried through the streets

on bamboo litters to the steps of the river, the waiting fires.
Barges float the river, loaded high with wood for the burnings.
Fire and water.

The burning must be done by Untouchables.
At the well for Untouchables children grab our hands.
All fire. All water.

SOMEBODY HAS MOVED THE BOUNDARY STONES

I don't know the name of this place.
The swollen tongue of it doesn't
fill its hungry cavity. We are so temporary
here with expiration dates stenciled like lace
on the nape of our necks. Naming
would give me slight modicum of control
but it escapes at the hollows of my throat.
Words fly away like fluff in the wind
before I can diagram them.
Any open door would be an invitation
to crawl through to a roiling
of atom, ion and atmosphere
careening between disordered boundaries
borrowed or broken to thud
where empty shirts hang heavy
in a cold wind, a storm brewing on the horizon.
I am trying to wash the stain out of a burned book.
I am a crane struggling to fly with my tiara
slipped down my stretched-out neck.
I am a long jade mirror catching
the image of the moon breathing
in the mists between myths.

ONCE

Once I lived in a forest
  and painted my face blue.

My children lived in stone barrows
  and kept rabbits in the house.

Once I sent them out on the ocean on a raft
  and tried to follow their trajectory as constellations of stars.

Once I saw your face, half in firelight, half in darkness
  cut right down the middle by refracted light.

We were on the beach that night,
  phosphorescence danced on the water like fireflies when we
    threw sand.

Once we walked on a pier where morning light slatted through our ribs
  and the silver fish of time swallowed itself.

The rain and wind had no meaning but rain and wind
  before it became compost and milk,
    loaves of bread rising.

Then a deep hole opened in the atmosphere and I fell in.

I worked at the Bakery of the Three Whores
  and the bread fell apart at the seams
    so nobody could eat it.

I tried to chant the world in shards of porcelain
    but it was a problem of translation.

Then I had no name
    but I tried to form one from hieroglyphs.
      in broken crockery
        found at the bottom of wells.

Once I lived in a book
    and went up in flames
      like scarves, like long strands of blown sand.

All the days were melon-colored, ranging to violet
    and you couldn't read in that light.

The letters kept re-arranging themselves into different words.
    They kept jutting out at odd angles.

J is the youngest, and still somewhat giddy,
    but the others are old enough to know better.

They are caught in amber, like bugs, like firelight,
    but change when you look at them from a different angle.

METAPHORS OF DUST

"We are stardust. We are golden."

As it turns out, we actually are stardust.
I thought it was a metaphor
of life and space and time.
Apparently, our materials are 13 million years old.
We are star stuff pondering the story
told in the life of the stars.

Our ancestors include imploded stars—
they are with us now, our dust,
we but continue the story
as additions, epilogues, a metaphor
for all that's been in this old
galaxy, the gravity of time .

Big balls of burning light and time
says the website of the stars.
How many millions of years old?
And we are made of all that dust
I can hardly tell now, what is not metaphor
and, literally, the story behind the story.

We are stardust pondering our own story.
We are spirit and story and caught in time
of existence as metaphor–
for what? That we are stars
and, like stars, will become dust
when we die old?

But it's so old,
this grand, often told story–
that we are dust and return to dust–
We are an instance of star in story
of rocks, glaciers, carbon-based creatures, stars.
We become the metaphor

and in this metaphor
we are all old
souls, stuff of ancient stars
singing our story
and whatever it says
about our mixture of spirit and dust.

We are the metaphor for the story
old souls swirling in the wind tunnel of time,
spirit and star and dust.

HOW IT IS

No tells *Can't* how it is with her.
"I'm not a book and you can't read me."
No shrugs her shoulders,
vanishing to a thin trick.

Ever follows *Never*'s bright footprints,
"Quit shadowing me," *Never*
echoes down stone walls
and escapes over fallen logs.

Possible closes the door of *Promise*
but lets a little light leak out,
a moon eaten nightly by sky,
but an answer, nonetheless.

To and *Fro* try escaping through tunnels
where twists still tangle in storm water sewers,
attracted helplessly to each other,
fall in love with *Gravity.*

Reflection falls down halls of self,
reverberating walls of sound,
a gong after it is struck,
echoing successive layers.

Maybe, progenitor
of *Yes*, turns toward *There*,
a slipshod unshod barefoot
territory, never *Here.*

HEAVEN

When I finally arrive there,
after a brief but mortal illness
I'll ask my mother which

great-great-grandma, picking spring flowers,
choked a bear with her own fist
shoved down his throat

and could it be true?
And for her recipe for turkey stuffing.
I'll be weeping just to see her again.

I'll tell her what I did
with the rest of my life,
that my later poems didn't have so much

sex, so she could have
shown them to her friends
without being embarrassed.

I'll let her know how the seeds of her stories
about Arthur and Guinevere,
Abelard and Heloise,

flamed at the heart of the Troubadour.
And that one of my children grew
up strong, though troubled

by the grief of life, and her very complexity,
and the other grew to become
a rare happy man, through his own complications.

And how bitter it became that I couldn't
ease their passage through the world.
She'll remember that as the bitter way of it,

how salmon and wolves
opened in me and she'll understand
with her own wild heart.

I'll tell her none of my marriages worked out
except for the children,
and that my sisters and I still seek

our misplaced childhood in each other,
in spite of how bossy I could be
as the first child.

I'll tell her that now I understand
what she meant, those many childhood nights
when I couldn't sleep, when she told me

it's all right, you are resting your heart.
I'll want to know if birds live there
and she'll name me their flaming colors.

And, I'm playing the piano again.
Haltingly at first, but I'm getting it back.
That will make her heart happy.

The world, I'll say, is still broken.
Ignorant armies clash by night,
and day, with less reason than the ones you knew.

She'll just nod, as if it's no longer her concern,
and perhaps it isn't. I will tell her
we are orphans in the presence of her absence.

And she'll tell me again
the story of the girl with flowers in her hands,
the Pomegranate seeds and the Underground.

PRAYER VIGIL
for Patricia Monaghan 1946-2012

If we are sad beyond knowing. We meet every evening in prayer time. Hold hands with our minds. It's a single idea but the days put on such reticence. Between pain and sleep and morphine. Between being happy when she is awake and relieved when she sleeps. When we were Pagan Mamas in Duluth many hatchet-faced women came to our reading ready to protest us, and we laughed about it later. I am 2,000 miles away. I would be in the way now. There, even he, her best beloved, could be in the way but his nearness eases her way. She is working so hard to do what she has to do. She's finding the base, her root of truth, this red-haired girl from the bog. Maybe she dreamed the world. She searches for breadcrumbs along the trail. Holding minds in hands from New York to Wisconsin, to the Arctic Circle, to Seattle grounds us. A cairn or two could point the way. Rock on rock. Eleven moose in one day on the Chena River, and more beaver than I could count. Are we past old stories? Is that part of the project here? She is in the process. She slips the surly bonds, this girl of the North. We hold minds in our hands. I heard about a three-masted schooner hovering just above the water for someone. "Look, look," he said. "I've never seen such a big ship on these waters before." No one else could see it but it sailed him away. Angels have come, someone for you beyond our kin. You will not be alone. The emptying of the house.

ABOUT SONG

> *yes! radiant lyre speak to me*
> *become a voice…*
>
> Sappho, fragment 118, tr. Anne Carson

The sound that springs
unbidden in hidden hot belief –
something will come to surprise
us, cloud unclouded,
a mound to sound angels of light
and we might finally know truth

and meaning of cruelty, dark blood,
bruising of innocents. News of rivers
singing in their downward journey,
curves and angles, geometries of history
sharp shape of tough questions
and why any god might choose

to strand us in this muddy eye
of wavering light, and yet, and yet,
and yet, astounding birds,
song, and possibility.

ALL FIRE ALL WATER is Judith Roche's fourth poetry collection. Her third, *Wisdom of the Body*, won an American Book Award and was nominated for a Pushcart Prize. She has published widely in various journals and magazines, and has poems installed on several Seattle area public art projects. She has written extensively about Pacific Northwest native salmon and edited *First Fish, First People: Salmon Tales of the North Pacific Rim*, for which she also received an American Book Award. Several of her salmon poems have been installed at the Hiram M. Chittendon Locks in Seattle. She has taught at numerous universities and currently teaches at Richard Hugo House Literary Center. She has conducted poetry workshops around the country. She is a Fellow in the Black Earth Institute, a progressive think tank exploring the links between nature, spirit, and social justice.